# LOVE

# Virus or Vaccine?

SANDEEP BOGRA

# Dedicated

To Everyone who's

*Infected* with Love !!

# Contents

# Preface

Every love story is unique, some filled with happiness, others marked by heartbreak. Despite its complexities, we continue to chase love, in our quest for 'someone special', hoping they will fulfill our deepest desires.

Love, one of the most powerful forces, is capable enough of both healing & hurting, giving joy & pain in equal measure, creating life-fulfilling experiences or leaving us scarred by disappointment.

What if love could be both?

A virus – an insidious force that germinates in our heart, spreads through our mind, and infects our soul, leaving us vulnerable to manipulation and control?

Or a vaccine – a healing force that heals our past wounds and preps us for the future, discovering our best version?

LOVE: Virus or Vaccine?

I explore this duality through Megha's journey.

A woman who loved deeply, lost painfully & struggled to trust again; Megha's heart discovered that how to love is a choice, it's a decision to choose someone consciously, but the outcome depends on multiple factors involved.

*This book, written with love, is structured around 8 chapters, each inspired by the 8 days of the Valentine's Week !*

This book is about understanding that love isn't a one-size-fits-all experience, reminding that we have the power to choose – the love we give & allow to let into our lives.

From the naive dreams of finding the perfect partner to the painful reality of toxic relationships, and the hope of healing through self-love and loving someone once again, this book emphasizes on the importance of choosing love with care and understanding, due to its evolving nature.

A must read for anyone who's never loved, someone who's been in love but lost, and for those who got hurt but ready to love again.

A story about self-discovery, healing, and growth – reemphasizing that love is not something to be afraid of or avoided, but something to be chosen wisely, with an intent to open our hearts to the possibility of connection, trust, love and care.

Love isn't a simple concept.

Is love a virus, something to be avoided, something that spreads and hurts? Or a vaccine, something to be embraced, the one that heals, strengthens and protects?

A question we need to ask for ourselves. While the answer isn't simple, but, it's worth discovering through this book.

# Acknowledgment

Immensely grateful to the Supreme Almighty…

He is always there, to take care, in our state of despair, with His guiding light, when nothing seems right !

*Life is the Best Teacher…*

Who knows it better than me!

Thank you, my dear life, for throwing challenges my way. Otherwise, I couldn't have learnt to overcome problems myself and assist others in their journey to success.

*I take this opportunity to salute all the love birds, who took a leap of faith, falling in love, and being with someone, forever…*

*Based on real-life, soul-stirring experiences of various couples, this book is a true reflection of their roller-coaster ride in love; I'm grateful to all these clients, who have been quite vocal in 'speaking their heart', adding life to this book.*

*Relationships, the biggest source of happiness & pain in my life, taught me a lot about myself and the world around me, and all the troubles I faced & overcame, made me a Relationship Coach.*

*After successful launch of two Bestseller books, 2021 & 2024, I'm delighted to gift this book of love to each one of you in 2025, on the eve of Valentine's Week, the time to celebrate — love…*

My deepest regards to all my teachers since childhood for their invaluable support always.

Sincere thanks to everyone believing in my abilities to transform their lives, from clients across the globe to former colleagues, friends, and followers.

After losing everyone forever, I thrive with the Heavenly blessings from my Parents and Grandparents.

My sister and extended family has always been around with their affection and warmth in my testing phase of life and deserve due recognition.

A special thank you to my lifeline – my friends, who are always so caring and concerned.

Much love to the reservoir of unconditional love I got in my life – my furry friend, my dog.

I owe it to each one of you...

# 1. Scent of a Rose

*"Mohabbat bhi zindagi ki tarah hoti hai…*

*Har mod aasaan nahi hota, har mod par khushi nahi hoti. Par jab hum zindagi ka saath nahi chhodte, toh mohabbat ka saath kyun chhodein?"*

(Love & Life are quite similar in many ways. Neither every turn is easy, nor every time does it bring happiness. But when we don't give up on life, then why give up on love?)

While this iconic dialogue from Shah Rukh Khan's Bollywood movie, *Mohabbatein*, reminds us of Aishwarya Rai Bachchan's views about love and life; this story revolves around someone named Megha, who was clueless about love, until…

***

From the very beginning, love was always something quire mysterious, something that whispered silent promises of fulfillment, a dream that existed in the spaces between dreams and reality, a fantasy, yet so real in her heart. A feeling like the strokes of soft brush of a rose's petals against her skin, light and almost ethereal, yet powerful enough to sweep her breath away.

For Megha, love was something she had always longed for – a long-term vision of beauty, a driving force that could fill her life with passion and joy, with meaning and a sense of completeness. It was a fragrant rose that symbolized all serenity, an experience enriched with purity and promise that she so desperately hoped to undergo someday.

Megha was always like the *Alice in Wonderland*, the type of girl to witness amusing situations, while seeing life through rose-tinted glasses. Her mind, ever since she was in her teens, was captivated by the idea of love – how it was spoken of so vividly in books, movies, and fairy tales.

Bollywood had always amplified her idea about love, where those lovely duos would dive in the ocean of love, only to swim through those soulful emotions of belongingness, and emerge stronger in bonding, which seemed to last beyond time. Ah well, that's how those romantic movies cloud our mind, affirming our beliefs about what love is all about – a state of permanence, a pillar of lifetime support, making our dreams come true !

Love is such a thing, isn't it?

A profound and complex emotion that defies an easy definition, a force that binds two individuals, transcending boundaries beyond time, shaping human connections in ways that are both mysterious and mystical. At its core, romantic love is all about connection, understanding and mutual experience between two unknown individuals.

Love, one of the most celebrated and intense feeling, often begins with attraction, followed by a deeper bond that builds over time, which encompasses both passion and commitment. The initial infatuation might bring moments of excitement and desire, but true romantic love deepens into a sense of belonging and mutual respect.

It requires effort and dedication to nurture over time, and it thrives on communication, trust, and a willingness to grow together, especially when going gets too difficult. Though love in a romantic sense is being vulnerable, opening oneself with all your insecurities and fears, risking up to both the potential for joy and the pain of heartbreaks, this vulnerability often strengthens the bond, creating a space for both partners to grow mutually.

Have you ever been in love ?

No matter how you relate to it, love is such a wonderful feeling, even words cannot describe so easily. Actually, you need to be in love to feel what love is all about…

It's what Megha firmly believed, as she loved those couple moments in the films and enjoyed watching them holding hands, as they strolled under the shimmering early-morning sun in the park across her house, smiling at each other, while sharing their innermost feelings in the kind of silence that spoke louder than words.

With a deep sigh, she would dream of the day when she too would experience a similar kind of perfect love. As an avid reader, every romance novel she devoured seemed to fill her with a bittersweet longing, the kind of yearning that made her ache for something she had never quite felt, yet so firmly believed she was meant to find.

Embracing the silence of the outer world, when the night was still and her thoughts could roam freely, Megha would close her eyes, only to visualize herself in the arms of a man who would cherish her, hold her close, not just physically, but emotionally, enwrap her in a way that would make her feel complete. Her senses imagined the scent of his perfume, the warmth of his loving embrace, the way his eyes would seem lost, while looking at her as someone who mattered most to him in the entire world. It was a fantasy that seemed to keep her awake all night, thumping her heart with ecstasy and joy, despite the overwhelming doubts creeping in sometimes.

Nevertheless, Megha's mind was always surmounted with love-filled clouds, reiterating the meaning of her name.

*(Megha is an Indian origin female name meaning — clouds.)*

Her mother often caught her staring out the window, a dreamy look on her face. "What are you thinking about, Megha?" she'd ask time and again, pretending to be unaware about her daughter's feelings, but for a reason. Megha, as always would smile, though it was a smile filled with a secret desire.

"I'm thinking about love, mummy," Megha would reply, in her soft and low voice.

Such response would always make her mother time-travel into her teens, when she was absorbed with the emotions of overflowing teenage love in college, with a handsome, young man, every girl would go weak in the knees at his mere sight.

Everyone isn't lucky in love, as they say!

Such was Megha's mother's belief, as she couldn't marry her college crush; hence worried so much about her daughter, who was so consumed with love.

Ignoring her past hurt of unmet desires, her mom would smile, rather chuckle, brushing her soft hands full of care and concern around Megha's face, every time she was thinking about love and always said – "Oh yes, love. It's a funny thing, isn't it? Something we all search for, yet so rare to find in real life. But when you finally get it, actually find it in real terms my darling Megha, it will be like the scent of a rose, so gentle and sweet."

Her mom's words stuck with Megha, lingering in her mind for years to come. *The scent of a rose.* Wow! She loved this unique way of looking at love, how it sounded, enveloping the delicate nature of love like rose, evoking feelings of both softness and soulfulness.

It became the foundation of Megha's belief about love – a love that would emerge someday in life, appear out of nowhere and fill her soul with beauty of companionship. She had always imagined love would be a natural occurrence, something that would bloom effortlessly, like rose petals blossom so vividly in the morning sunshine.

Beliefs in our infancy stage play a crucial role in shaping our adult relationships. From the moment we're born, we begin to internalize messages about love, affection and how relationships should function. Such experiences in our early age or the environment around us influence how we perceive ourselves and others romantically.

Our parents' married life also impacts our expectations in adulthood as they become our role model. A child who witnesses conflict resolution, empathy and compromise in relationships is more likely to replicate these behaviors in their romantic life. Conversely, if they observe unhealthy patterns like anger or emotional withdrawal, these patterns may carry over into their adult love lives.

Ultimately, childhood beliefs about love form the foundation for how we engage in and experience love…

Time passed by and Megha's idea of love became more profound, while the essence remaining unchanged.

Love seemed pure and serene, something to be cherished forever. She dreamt of the day when someone would look at her with the same admiration she had seen in the couples on the big screen, someone who would sweep her off her feet and make her feel adored like the most invaluable person in their world.

But as she entered her late teens, reality began to shift her perspective. Her first crush was intoxicating. He was tall, with curly black hair and a smile too good to resist. They had met during a festival celebration in their society, and every moment spent around him felt like the world had slowed down just for her.

After all, Megha was sunk in love !

This guy would glance through her soul, peeping deep inside her heart, while Megha skipped her heartbeat in his presence. She could almost hear the bells ringing, as if everything around them had faded away, leaving both suspended somewhere, with love in the air.

For the first time in her life, she felt like living inside the dream, that fantasy she always held close to her heart seemed true.

It's when the reality set in. The short-lived situationship was full of excitement at first, but soon the cracks began to appear. Their dreams and future plans seemed misaligned. Megha found herself questioning what was happening so swiftly in her life, unable to comprehend the sudden changes from infatuation to a casual romance, followed by his disappearance from her life so soon.

This incident left an impact on her heart, mind and soul. The rose which seemed so sweet wasn't alluring after all.

She witnessed a shift in her own identity, as she questioned herself while standing in front of the mirror – was it love or something else? Was she even meant for it?

Still, she couldn't ignore the feeling that real love existed somewhere, hidden for the time being, yet to be unfolded by the universe at the right time, with the right person, meant for her; the chosen one. She made herself understand that she needs to be patient with life.

How can something the world talks about in movies and novels be a myth? Real love does exist, she reminded herself daily.

The scent of a rose dipped in love was still blooming in her heart. Megha believed that love would find her way eventually, when his perfect partner would make everything fall into place, who would shower love upon her in the way she had always imagined.

It wasn't until a few experiences of short-lived relationships shared by her friends, that Megha realized – love didn't just happen by accident. It didn't simply appear one fine day like the spring season, when a perfect rose would fall into her lap.

*Real love isn't like Reels on social media, it's different from Virtual Reality (VR) as it requires lots more than mere imagination or what could Artificial Intelligence (AI) do in creating those unreal transition effects, nowhere close to real challenges life's circumstances have to offer on the path of love ! Even Chat GPT can't bring out those real emotions to surface.*

Megha was no longer the naive girl who believed love would fix everything. In fact, she had become more cautious and aware of the nuances of relationships. She understood that love wasn't always going to be like the gentle scent of a rose. Sometimes, it could be like a thorn, pricking her gentle heart, leaving behind scars that wouldn't heal so easily.

Still, her dreams continued…

One afternoon, while walking through a mall, Megha came across a florist's stall. The scent of roses immediately engulfed her senses, filling the air with its sweet and intoxicating fragrance, just as she had always imagined. She stood still for a while, as she picked up a rose, with its soft and delicate petals merging with her pink cheeks, as she held it close to her face.

For a moment, she was lost somewhere, as she felt what always seemed so familiar – the hope that love, in all its glory, was still waiting for her. That one fine day, her dreams would turn into reality.

But for now, she just felt like holding that rose close to her heart, symbolic of her dreams, her fantasies, the love she was yet to find. The scent of a rose would always remind her of infinite possibilities, if she kept holding on to her belief that love was worth waiting for.

As she walked away from the stall, the rose clutched in her hand so tight, like holding on to her dreams forever. She was yet to realize that love in real terms, would be far more complicated than she could ever imagine.

After all, you need to deal with its thorns, while you hold its bunch and savour the sweet, floral and slightly spicy

*Scent of a Rose...*

# 2. Chose to Propose

Life moved on and Megha's focus shifted towards her career. She was busy developing her skillset to take advantage of the upcoming opportunities in the professional sphere, unaware what life had in store for her.

Amidst all the tight deadlines allocated by her boss, she decided to attend her friend's housewarming party, the invitation to something warm and magical experience, waiting for her as a surprise.

As she entered her friend's villa on Sunday evening, she found herself surrounded by a sea of faces wherein a tall, dark and handsome guy seemed to grab everyone's attention.

When Megha first met Aryan, there was something magnetic about him. He had an effortless charm, someone who seemed to light up a room just like that.

It wasn't just his cute smile, though it was undoubtedly infectious, but his confidence and calm, the ease with which he carried on his conversations, making everyone feel like they were the most important person in the room. And for Megha, his charm was like a lighthouse in the sea, a lifeguard in the midst of high tides of emotional upheaval, a beacon in the darkness of her uncertainties, drawing her closer towards him, making her feel heard and seen in ways she hadn't felt before.

Aryan was exactly the kind of personality Megha had imagined herself with ever since she had those dreamy nights – charming, confident, funny, wise and responsible enough to take care of her lows and highs.

He swept her off her feet, just as she had always imagined a man would. With his conscious deep gaze, he had an unusual ability to make her feel special, like she was the only woman out there, exactly what Megha had been longing for her entire life.

In the early stages of their relationship, everything felt like a dream. An instantaneous connection, like they had known each other forever. Long overnight calls, spending hours talking about their hopes, dreams and future.

Aryan was her *"Someone Listening"* with all the willingness to tune into her soul, an attentiveness she had rarely experienced, while offering insights that made her feel heard and understood. What else could a girl ask for…

And when they came closer in person, Aryan's touch, whether holding her with his arms around her waist or a brief brush of their fingers, it felt electric, like the sparks of a fire waiting to ignite, something too irresistible. For Megha, this was everything she had imagined love to be – so effortless, passionate, full of spark and delight, seeming like dreams willing to see the light of the day.

She couldn't help but be swept up in the whirlwind of it all. It was as if all the books, those romantic movies, the lovely songs she had ever consumed had culminated in this one, magical moment with the man in her life.

Oh my God ! What is happening to me? Exclaimed Megha in a surprise, as she went down the memory lane !

Despite her idealistic tendencies, Megha had always remained cautious. We know she had been burned before. The scars from her past situationship were still visible in her present moments, reeling at the back of her mind. She knew love was fragile, to be handled with extra caution.

While she could barely resist the magnetic pull between her and Aryan, she kept herself away at an arm's length distance, wary of letting her guard down so soon. There were questions that lingered at the back of her mind, disallowing herself to open up, as her past reality threatened the dream she had already started to build in this present moment with Aryan.

While her career graph was rising high, so was her state of emotions and tension simultaneously. She was caught daydreaming about the man in her life, mindful enough not to miss her deadlines in office though, still being ignorant of her work sometimes.

Was it a good thing to become careless as she rose up the corporate ladder? I wonder if she ever bothered much.

"Is he too good to be true? What if I'm just caught up in the fantasy of it all?" It's what she was actually concerned about and asked herself silently every night, while falling deeper into his soulful whispers on phone.

Still, the pull of his seductive presence was undeniable, and soon, they were inseparable. They had plans together, dreams building up, with their future shaping up. Aryan was quick to admit how he felt about her and spoke of love with such confidence, as it was something destined to happen between the two of them. He was open and honest, daring and direct, passionate and pleasing. Every time he was around, she felt she was the one he had been waiting for his entire life.

As they sat together on her couch, watching the sunset over the dimming sky, with her girly instincts, Megha looked into his eyes with a feeling of uneasiness, wondering as if something unusual was about to happen.

"I love you, Megha," said Aryan, as he cupped her face, looking into her twinkling eyes, holding her by surprise !

His confession came quite easily with such a conviction, without any doubt on his mind, as he seemed crystal clear about the feelings he shared for her.

But Megha, despite the flutter in her chest, felt quite hesitant and uneasy. Was it so early to hear those three magical words? Was it too soon for her to believe him? She had realized in her past that love, when rushed through could be a dangerous game to play with.

While she wanted to believe Aryan, maybe she truly did, but there was a voice deep inside her, raising concerns for her future, that urged her to exercise utmost caution. That voice from her past, reminded of the mistakes she had made around getting into such encounters which started out of nowhere, only to crumble those promises which once seemed so true to pour one's heart for.

Now she was in a fix, something even love couldn't fix !

While love had always been an elusive dream, something she had been chasing since teenage, she was perplexed whether she should embrace it or let go of the love, which was right there in front of her? Was it wrong to let herself let loose or protect her heart with a shield of security?

Trust it isn't easy for anyone, especially in love, when you're at such crossroads in life, burdened with the uncertainty of unknown future on either side, clueless which way to move ahead, as *falling* in love isn't easy, so isn't the pain of *failing* therein !

FOMO or the Fear of Missing Out, has seeped into relationships nowadays to the extent that individuals fall into the trap of anxiety to form connections, which may not be genuine or ripe enough yet. Watching others flaunting a happy relationship on social media further creates a societal pressure and undue expectations from oneself, urging us to get tagged with someone special.

While Megha was juggling with work deadlines in office, her personal life was raising an alarm to do something quickly, as her friends had started getting married now.

But she was still hesitant to move ahead, something she struggled to understand. Aryan seemed perfect on paper. He had everything what life had to offer. He was successful in his career, building his wealth while enjoying his passion to travel, especially road trips in his 4x4.

Raised in a family well known in uppermost strata of the society, with friends who adored him and a personality full of confidence that made him appear strong and capable. He had an aura too good to resist.

But as their relationship progressed, Megha had a bizarre feeling that something wasn't quite right. Aryan was neither cruel nor abusive, rather was quite the opposite. He was extremely caring, very attentive, and too affectionate. But there were those moments that made Megha feel somewhat uneasy, with subtle hints that maybe things weren't as good as it seemed.

He would belittle her friends with strong comments, showing his supremacy in understanding her better than everyone known to her before she met him, as if they weren't as important as he was, considering himself as the only one who matters in her life. Even during arguments, he often brushed her feelings aside, stating that she was simply overreacting and she seemed too sensitive.

Megha kept telling herself that it was just the teething issues of a new relationship, just small misunderstandings. But deep down inside, she couldn't ignore her voice that whispered – "It doesn't feel right."

Nevertheless, every time Megha felt her doubt creeping in, Aryan would turn the tables by doing something to make her feel special, way more than before.

If you love me, love my dog.

While Megha never asked for such kind of love, he would display it to her, making everyone delighted in her small little world. He would bring her flowers for no reason, send a special cake and gifts for everyone at her home on their birthdays, reflect his care and concern if anyone fell ill, send her texts throughout the day telling her how much he missed her, and take her on spontaneous date nights or outings that left her breathless with excitement.

His charm was so compelling that every time she began to question her feelings for him, Aryan would draw her back, like those magnetic opposite poles.

But in those quiet moments, when she wasn't absorbed in the thrill of this relationship, she would reflect upon what was going around her and those questions returned.

Was he trustworthy? The right person to build a future with? Or was she falling for the fantasy of love rather than the reality of life?

One evening, they were sitting in his car, parked on the roadside, with car indicators blinking faster than usual, resembling those palpitations Megha felt in her heart. While she had always found comfort in the stillness of these quiet moments, with stars shimmering in the clear night sky, but tonight, her thoughts were clouded.

"I've been thinking about us nowadays Megha," said Aryan in his soft voice. "I firmly believe we're meant to be together oh dear. I love you and wish you be my partner, for the rest of our lives."

Megha's heart skipped a beat but something felt uneasy. She looked at him, clueless what to say, as the tension and fear burning inside began to surface, irrespective of his genuine, heartfelt and reassuring words.

"Aryan," she replied, "I care about you, trust I really do. But I'm not so sure about a long-term relationship yet, as I need to know if this is more than just a momentary feeling and we're not rushing into something because it feels good to be so around each other."

"Oh Megha, I've thought about this a lot now. Trust, I don't wish to waste our time. You and I, we make sense. I want you in my life and am pretty sure about it," said Aryan, as he held Megha's hand gently yet firm, while drawing it closer to his heart and placing on his chest.

His words were like a soothing balm, relieving her of the anxiety building inside her, and his touch seemed so caring for the delicate girl, she was trying to protect inside her. But at the same time, this surreal experience intensified her internal struggle. Her heart and mind pulling her in two opposite directions; with her heart pulling her to believe that this was the love she had been waiting for and her mind pushing her away, raising an alarm and saying that love was something to be chosen wisely, not merely felt. Love must be a wise decision, a conscious choice.

Now this was getting very tricky for her, as on the one side, she knew she couldn't make that choice out of desperation and on the other hand, how could she walk away from someone who seemed so perfect for her? A decision of life she had to be certain about, that she wasn't being swept away by the wave of emotions stirred by Aryan in her mind.

But it wasn't going to be easy, as how could she tell him that despite all the positives, there was a part of her that wasn't ready to take the leap of faith? How could she explain that while she loved the way he made her feel, she needed something more to be so sure?

"I need time, Aryan," Megha said, in her voice too low, fearing his unknown reaction.

To her surprise, he looked at her with a smile, though this time, the smile didn't quite connect with her heart !

"While I understand your concern, just remember, time may not be our side always," he said quietly yet firmly.

His words felt quite heavy for Megha, who kept wondering if he truly understood what she meant. She wasn't asking for more time to decide if she loved him; she already knew she did. She just wanted more time to decide if this love could be the love of her lifetime.

As she walked out of his car that night, the emotions of love & doubt, hope & fear kept swirling in her heart. She knew she won't rush through emotions this time, as it was about making the right choice.

It was a matter of her life…

The confusion wasn't if she was ready to propose, but whether he was the one, sent by the universe, whom she could trust to love forever, someone she could build a future with for the sunset years; so, she could look back in time and feel proud that he was the best one ever, she

*Chose to Propose…*

# 3.  The Dark Chocolate !!

Girls love chocolates, isn't it?

Especially when a guy wraps it with all his love and care, an expression of his affection.

Chocolates and love seem intertwined in a sensory experience, as there's always something magical when a chocolate melts in your mouth, with your tongue tasting its smoothness like a delicate kiss, unfolding in love. Elevating your soul with its power, love like chocolate awakens the senses within. Such connection between the two is not just about indulgence; it's about creating a special bond, a shared meaningful experience that brings people closer and keeps them together, forever.

That night when Megha stepped out of the car, Aryan had placed a chocolate wrapped in a love letter in her purse. His warmth of love melted her heart, soft like chocolate, and she accepted his proposal, finally…

"I never thought I'd feel this way. For so long, I was skeptical of love, wondering if it could only leave me disappointed. But then, it just happened, and I feel you're the one I've been waiting for oh my Aryan," said Megha on her first ever video call that night itself.

She went on further to share so much hidden deep inside. "I remember it started with a glance in that housewarming party, a spark leaving us delighted together in love, dipped in the molten chocolate, full of softness like raisins, a distinct crunch and richness of nuts, much like unique experiences yet to unfold in our journey, with the base so smooth and velvety chocolate, representing our depth of closeness."

She had never imagined someone would amaze her with everything she wanted, yet feared if she would get it at all. And yet, here she was, feeling surprised for herself, as she never thought she'd let herself believe in love, trust, hope, and maybe even a little bit of magic.

With every conversation and shared laugh, she let go of the walls built around her heart. Sweet and tender like chocolate, this newfound connection was a new beginning for Megha, who discovered a side of herself she had simply forgotten.

Love isn't something to fear, but to rejoice, as its perfect and real, utmost beautiful thing she'd never expected.

Was it so?

It had only been a few months since Megha made up her mind to be with Aryan. She had taken that leap of faith, believing that real love was worth all the risks. She had chosen to trust him blindly, allowing herself to fall into a relationship that seemed so perfect.

But in no time, she began to notice that things weren't as sweet as she had imagined. The scent of the fragrant rose had begun to fade, their relation lacked its sweetness of love, leaving behind something darker and bitter, like a piece of dark chocolate.

Aryan, the charmer, like chameleon, started to show his true colors. While Megha reassured herself he wasn't bad, but there was definitely something about him that made her uneasy. His warm words of affection and care had slowly transformed into something cold and more distant.

It was like the darkness of the chocolate had taken over. It was all cocoa without sugar to balance it out. And as Megha's relationship with Aryan deepened, she felt herself drawn into a world opposite to her dreams. It was a place filled with strange acts of manipulation, control and subtle cruelty. She started feeling it with every act and gesture of him, neither loud nor overt, but it was there, as every small thing Aryan did, slowly chipped away her identity.

The middle class Megha found herself lost in the middle of everything Aryan had to offer, coming from a space lacking in love but full of superiority, to rule everyone, including the one in his life.

The early signs that something wasn't right came in the form of an argument, a small and insignificant one about something trivial. Megha had suggested a romantic comedy movie, something lighthearted, to cheer up. Aryan, however, kept insisting on watching a thriller, intense and dark like his personality underneath his charismatic smile.

"I'm not in the mood for a rom-com," Aryan said, his tone more dismissive and overpowering. "Grow up Megha, you aren't in college anymore."

Now this might sound funny to feel odd about a movie genre, but such subtle signs of ignorance have been present across generations, making one feel unimportant, unheard and unworthy. Over time, such relationships begin to crack under the weight of unmet expectations from one's partner.

At this instance, Megha's first instinct was to back down, as she always kept him on priority. She didn't want to upset him or the relationship, but the way he spoke certainly irritated her. It felt like her preferences didn't matter, as if he was trying to control everything, the way she thought, felt, choices she made and things she wanted.

"Umm, I'm in the mood for a rom-com Aryan," she said, in a trembling voice. "Can we watch it today?"

With eyes rolled up, he replied, "Why are you always so difficult? Stop acting like a child."

A small comment from Aryan, a giant blow for Megha !

Megha tried to get over it, telling herself it was nothing. But the feeling of being uneasy continued, a growing knot in her stomach, telling her something wasn't right.

Repetition is the mother of all problems, when similar patterns continue, without failing to understand and address the underlying issues. Such was her ongoing experience with Aryan, who would make subtle remarks at everything she shared, including her choices, opinions, dressing sense and style of communication, stating it didn't really match to her level or the company of friends he had, while always demeaning her set of companions, who always wanted to meet her boyfriend but Aryan would always deny on one pretext or the other, with his underlying thought that her friends weren't the right kind of people to be around. It wasn't overtly controlling, but enough to make Megha second-guess herself and her choices, making her feel small, insignificant, as her self-worth was defined by Aryan's approval.

The dark chocolate in their relationship was taking over, melting the real essence of love they started with.

While it's natural to behave naturally around the ones you share your life with, being raw and cold towards your significant other, without empathy under the guise of your personality or mindset isn't justified, especially when you chased them to be yours and they took time to choose…

It wasn't just those little comments but acts of control, which Megha began to notice every time things didn't go according to Aryan's plan. When they argued, he would often stonewall her and shut down, giving her the cold shoulder or zoning into his silence retreat, ignoring her for days, without caring at all how such cruel yet consistent behavior was carving impressions of hurt and pain on Megha's mind, someone he craved for until she accepted his proposal, and now, all he would gift her in return was nothing but lack of understanding and unwillingness to work through their issues.

He wouldn't explain himself or try either, instead, he would pull away, leaving Megha wondering and guilty about what wrong she had done. Every time she made an earnest attempt to discuss their problems, Aryan would avoid being *Someone Listening*, but respond with harsh words that left her feeling more hurt and confused.

Sometimes in life, all you need – *Someone Listening.*

Someone, with whom you can speak your heart, express yourself, in a safe, non-judgmental environment. You aren't looking for an advice to resolve things, but certainly have the underlying urge to feel heard & understood, that you matter, and there's Someone to lend you their listening ear and make you believe they are there for you, when everything you're feeling or going through is crucial for you to address and maintain basic relationship sanity.

Its all Megha was yearning from Aryan, but…

"You're always overthinking," he'd rather say, while dismissing everything Megha brought up for discussion. "Why can't you just relax?" Aryan kept complaining.

How could she relax, when he never helped her being so? How could she just go with the flow, when her emotions were overflowing and her feelings being stomped upon, opinions and suggestions being dismissed, and her identity put to question. Her situationship in the past was different, minimal in terms of what she was going through. She wasn't just hurt, she felt invisible.

Self-doubt started creeping in Megha's mind.

Was she being too sensitive or just imagining such things? After all, Aryan loved her, of course he did or he didn't? He confessed it and showed up in ways so true to believe. Expressing it in numerous ways like spending time with her in all those fancy places, buying her expensive gifts, evenings spent at royal gatherings with his set of people, telling her how much he cared in his own ways. But every gesture came with strings of obligations attached.

"I love you" rarely felt a genuine expression, as the core need of being *Someone Listening* was missing throughout.

She felt like walking on eggshells, avoiding doing or saying anything on her mind that would upset him. Heartfelt conversations were out of window since long.

Her dreamy relationship with Aryan now felt like a trap.

In her futile attempt to make him understand, she felt pushed back and eventually lost herself. All that made her feel amazing in the past like spending time with her friends, pursuing her dreams and hobbies, working passionately in her career, or just relaxing by herself was buried under the weight of pleasing Aryan, which she couldn't. Still, nothing seemed to help.

"Why nothing seems to work nowadays?" asked Megha from her mother, the one who had seen her dreaming every night under the stars, waiting for love to shine in her life. Her mom was undoubtedly her bestie since childhood, who saw her growing through different phases of life's emotions, like waxing & waning moon in the sky.

Her mom had a simple logic and reasoning behind relationship failures – Failing to choose is choosing to fail.

Unfortunately, majority of us like Megha, fail to choose our partners wisely, thereby ensuring chaos later on.

So, why does this happen, you might wonder, right?

What if I told you that our school, college, society, even family and friends have taught us everything in life, except *how to do relationships…*

Yes, you read it right ! Relationships never work by mere existence of two people coming together, but with all the work they put in to sustain and grow their bond with time.

*Relations, unlike airplanes, never run on autopilot !*

So, whose fault it was in such a strained relationship?

I'm sure everyone will believe it was Aryan's ugly behavior leading to catastrophe. Maybe or maybe not?

Did Megha hurried to fall in love with him (a wrong choice as per her mother's profound logic behind relationship failures) or started with a wrong set of expectations or something else? Or the lack of understanding about how to handle relationships on part of Aryan or both leading to disaster?

Failing to understand the root cause, Megha simply realized how far the relationship had gone off track. While she could no longer ignore the growing discomfort, the hope things might get fine vs. the sense that something was deeply wrong, kept her thinking.

Their relationship, once so alluring, had turned into something not so yummy anymore.

Megha realized that everything in life – the taste of dark chocolate and someone's bitter personality was a matter of one's personal interests, which differed for everyone.

Those who liked it, loved its rich flavor, so dark and intense., inviting one's taste buds to explore more refined and deeper experiences, without much sweetness. For everyone else, without much sugar, it was just unpalatable, due to its bitterness, increasing with every bite, making it difficult to have it anymore.

Aryan's love, like the dark chocolate, seemed to have depth in the beginning, full of intense emotions, passion for his partner, which commanded undue attention.

While every girl might have longed for tasting it, Megha was the lucky one (at least according to Aryan), which came at a price, her own self-identity. So, when she took a bite, she realized that it lacked sweetness, the care and warmth that made love feel safe and fulfilling. Instead, it left a bitter experience, one she couldn't quite shake.

Girls love chocolates, isn't it?

Remember, I asked you in the start?

Well, in a relationship, I'm sure they won't, especially when a guy extracts the sweet essence out of it, fills it up with ingredients like control, ignorance and disrespect, and wraps it with all his superficial love (an expression of his negative personality), leaving behind a bitter taste like

*The Dark Chocolate !!*

# 4.  Teddy… Ready… Go…

*Koi pyaar kare toh tumse kare, tum jaise ho waise kare… Koi tumko badal ke pyaar kare, toh woh pyaar nahi, woh sauda kare… Aur saheba, pyaar mein sauda nahi hota. Right?*

(If someone loves you, they should love you, as you are. If someone wants to change you to become worthy of your love, then it's not love, but a bargain. Ah well, there's no deal in love. Right?)

Yet another iconic dialogue from Shah Rukh Khan's Bollywood movie, *Mohabbatein*, talks about the basic principle of love, that you must accept your partner as s/he is, else you're not really in love with that person !

***

For the first time, Megha realized Aryan's true personality, a person who didn't love her the way she was, rather how he wanted to change her to tune into him. Trust it wasn't going to work in the long run. After all, how could she sustain in a place of constant denial of love she deserved.

He wasn't the real charming, perfect partner she found. He was someone who wanted constant control, who couldn't love her without undermining her, as he always considered himself superior to her in every aspect, while Megha was tired of making herself understand that he wasn't like that, pretending that everything was okay when it really wasn't.

The final blow came on an evening that started off like any other day. A normal conversation turned into a heated argument, flaring up emotions, leading to a never-ending exchange of hateful words from both sides. Yes, Megha opened up, finally, as the volcano deep inside her busted. While she always tried to compromise in the past and he shut her down every time, she didn't want to give in to his undue dominance this time.

When the argument escalated, Aryan's anger became more apparent. His voice raised and suddenly he hit her across her face and Megha, in a sudden shock, felt like she was dealing with a narcissist, not the one she had loved.

Aryan was no more a lover but a stranger !

The coldness in his eyes and the harshness in his words might have led her to hang in there for some more time but the blow across her face was too much to handle.

For the first time, Megha wasn't being indecisive (while Aryan always considered her so), as she was very clear what she was going to do now. She was done with him, but he needed to learn a lesson, before she parted ways.

"You think the world revolves around you? Well, then you're highly mistaken Mr. Aryan. You think you can make the world dance to your tunes with your flamboyant lifestyle, girls might fall for? Well, then you're with a wrong person. And let me tell you something you need to beware about – any such girl who falls for your money, will eventually be the reason for your downfall. Mind it."

Megha was on fire, as she said it all, in a firm and loud voice, while recollecting herself, giving it back on his face.

The words hit Aryan harder than she expected. There was a pin-drop silence, as he stared at her in stunned disbelief, yet unable to utter a word anymore in front of her. Megha's clouds of anger burst like a thunderstorm, which he couldn't handle. He had never imagined a soft-spoken girl would thrash her so badly.

While she was always wrong in his eyes until now, it didn't matter anymore, as she knew nothing would help revive the lost trust or love anymore. This chapter was over…

As the days passed, Megha withdrew from Aryan. She stopped responding or reaching out, blocked him on social media and everywhere, as she realized she couldn't continue living like this. The relationship had turned from something sweet and promising to something bitter and suffocating. The sweetness of love of her dreams was now taken over by the bitterness of Aryan's reality.

It was in those moments, as she lied down in her bed, quiet in the middle of the night, gazing at the stars like always; just this time, she wasn't dreaming anymore, but grasping the most important lessons of lifetime she had learnt recently.

Her mother saw this vulnerability in her eyes but avoided disrupting her processing of emotions, so crucial for her.

Love wasn't meant to pull her down, rather lift her spirits, make her feel confident, do away her pain than feeling like a constant struggle. It wasn't supposed to leave her questioning her self-worth, which seemed corroded in Aryan's love like rust.

That night, Megha went into the self-introspection mode. Trust it wasn't easy, and of course it didn't come without tears, but it was the only choice she was left with. She was done with the dark side of love, full of manipulation, control and insecurity.

This isn't what she came for…

Leaving Aryan behind wasn't so easy as she imagined.

Megha had thought it would be the hardest thing to do, but it became more evident that the most difficult thing will be something else, as she walked away from their relationship. It was the emotional aftermath, with her self-worth being demolished and the painful process of picking up those shattered pieces.

The realization that love wasn't always something you could simply walk away from was far more than a mere feeling passing by, as it lingered on in the middle of everything running on her mind while at work, in the quiet spaces of her heart when she lied down in the silent night, stirring emotions when she least expected.

Megha was like a teddy bear, soft at her core, gentle, kind, and always caring and comforting, especially to those she loved. But Aryan had torn away that layer of softness, testing her limits, while she kept on hoping and waiting for him to be somewhat gentle towards her feelings.

She had always believed that love was worth fighting for, no matter the cost, which turned out to be very expensive. She gave in so much of herself, only to get nothing in return but emptiness and void from a coward like Aryan, which was too difficult to fill in, as she had lost all hope to hope anything now.

*"The biggest coward of a man is to awaken the love of a woman without the intention of loving her." – Bob Marley*

After the breakup, Megha withdrew from everything and everyone around, just lost into herself. While she cut-off all ties with Aryan, for her own well-being, the teddy bear inside her needed to heal. But only time could help her.

Those were the most challenging days of her life, when everything felt so hard. She had taken sick leave from office as she could barely manage her daily chores. Every morning, she woke up feeling quite heavy, as if something was missing, like her soul had been ripped out.

But as the days went by, she started feeling that she had to reclaim herself, to avoid dwelling in the past forever, to pull out from Aryan's dark shadow looming over herself. It was time to let go of whatever had happened with her, to stop being a victim in her own eyes, and start taking control of her inner dialogue, to recreate her new story.

Healing wasn't easy, it never really is.

But Megha was strong and sensible enough to take action. She had learnt from someone about life & relationship coaching and decided to give it a shot, hoping it helps. To her surprise, it was a real eye-opener to new possibilities and a new future. Of course, she had to continue working on herself, with the tools and strategies guided by her coach, to eventually get results. It was a journey she had to take, with guidance and support of a professional, who could help her transform, only to the extent of her willingness to seek help and rise like a phoenix…

One afternoon, Megha sat on the couch in her balcony, while sipping her tea, in the cold weather inside-out.

Megha was convinced that she was done with love. She couldn't withstand the very idea of being in love again. Why would she risk her heart going through pain now? Why let the doors to hell open, when the one she trusted to take care of her heart, had already left her heartbroken?

Her thoughts were interrupted by a bang on the door. Megha stood up wondering, as her mom was away and she wasn't expecting anyone at this time. Don't know why, but she thought it was Aryan, just the way he would always be hitting the door, giving last minute surprises. Hesitant to open, she peeped through the door eye. Surprisingly, it wasn't him, but her best friend, Myra.

"Myra? Oh my God !" Megha screamed, taken aback by her unexpected visit.

Myra gave her the hug of a lifetime, something she was so missing, ever since she had lost herself.

"I thought you might need me to stay with you for a few days," she said, stepping inside without an invitation.

What else are real friends for, to pop-in in your life and hold you strong, when you're falling apart, to be your pillar of support.

"You're a life-saving drug," said Megha, taking the bag from her. "Even I didn't know how much I needed you."

Megha smiled a little, after countless days, feeling a rush of gratitude for Myra, who always knew how to make her feel good and pull her out of her darkest moments.

The two friends nested in the couch, eating and chatting around everything they had cherished together since school times, while carefully avoiding talking about anything related to Aryan and the painful experiences leading to breakup. Myra didn't want her to talk about it, as she knew Megha needed that urgent cut-off from those painful memories, before she felt willing enough to speak.

Nevertheless, Myra always had that ongoing concern reflecting in her eyes, that her friend might never fully recover, burdened with the immense pain of heartbreak.

After a few days, said Myra, in her very serious voice, "You know Megha, I've been thinking a lot about you all these days, ever since Aunty told me about everything." "I know it's been a big toll on your life, but you can't let this one breakup define who you really are. You're still that cute, lovely teddy bear at your core, that innate quality of being a lovely soul. And no one can steal it from you."

A gentle reminder about who she was, even after all that had happened, is what Megha really needed at this point.

"I don't know if I can be myself again," Megha replied, absorbing this sudden dose of exhilarating motivation, though insufficient to revive someone lost and dead deep inside like Megha.

"You're not empty, Megha, you can never be so dear," Myra responded firmly. "Time is the biggest healer. No need to rush into anything. Just avoid shutting yourself off completely, that's it."

Megha went quite but her mind racing, resonating deeply with Myra's words. Maybe for the first time in weeks, Megha felt a small ray of hope. Maybe she wasn't completely broken after all. Hopefully, with time, she would learn to love again, if not someone else, but herself.

With all those exercises suggested by her life coach, Megha started to focus on herself again, all those small things that made her feel happy. She went for long walks in the same park, where she used to see couples walking, started painting, that always brought her comfort, started reconnecting with her friends. Slowly, she started feeling alive, the real version of herself she had almost forgotten.

As she rebuilt herself, Megha couldn't shake the feeling that something was still missing. Though she had made peace with being single, part of her still hoped that one day, life would change, that someday, love might return, not from Aryan of course, but someone, who made sense.

She wasn't desperate for love anymore, as she knew self-love ought to be her priority, to fill in the void inside, before she could expect anyone else to fill in the blanks. Her reservoir of self-love was vital to be replenished, only then she could imagine to gift it to someone in future…

Megha finally made a vow to herself, that she would never allow her past define her present and spoil her future.

She might take time to heal, but she would, while gathering all her hidden strength, embracing the reality of life and never give up. She will rediscover herself and the ability and willingness to love again, first with the inner child, sitting quiet and afraid inside her, and then, someone, who might get lucky to have her.

The scratch of thorns, which came with those fragrant roses, seemed to disappear. She was ready to let go of the bitterness of the dark chocolate and bask in something sweet like self-love, which was soft like a teddy bear, yet turning her strong enough to protect her heart.

The next chapter of her life was ready to unfold, as Megha was no longer afraid of life. After all, she had faced a lot already. She was open to the possibility of healing, believing that *true love wasn't about perfection but inner-reflection*, finding the courage to love herself first, then allowing her soul to become one with "Special Someone." Megha was ready to take off, as she said to her inner child

*Teddy… Ready… Go…*

# 5.  The Real Promise

It was early spring when Megha decided that it was time for her heart to breathe again, just like the spring season, an awakening from the dark, cold winter nights, when the nature hits the reset button, and everything becomes alive again, with a renewed hope and perspective about life, letting go of things that no longer serve any purpose, making room for new beginnings, with endless possibilities of growth in future.

Megha had come a long way. She had spent last so many months healing herself from the toxicity of past relationship, pulling back together one piece at a time.

Still, there was something missing. Love and connection, a basic human need, was always unmet in her life. Despite the healing, there was a part of her that desired for genuine love, an experience that would make her feel complete, something she had once believed would fall in her lap.

She had kept the doors to her heart shut since so long, too afraid to let anyone knock or enter therein. But after weeks of introspection and self-discovery, Megha understood that she couldn't keep herself imprisoned in life, that she couldn't keep her heart locked away forever. She wasn't ready to dive into a relationship so soon, but wanted to open herself to the possibility of being alive, promising herself never to rush in making the right choice.

*It was a new world, a fresh start, time for Megha 2.0*

The first thing she did was that she decided to rebuild her confidence, with her newfound independence from the past and sheer determination to build a better tomorrow. She had wasted her life relying on others to validate her emotions, her personality and had lost herself in the process. She had given up herself, trying to fit into someone else's world, giving up her own dreams, to match their reality, which she never could. Actually, nobody can. Now, it was time to take it back, reset her mindset, learn to unlearn the wrong software her mind was coded with, rebuild her self-worth, more than her net worth.

Her coach had been instrumental in guiding her through the transformation process. He was the one reminding her that she didn't need a partner to define her worth or give her happiness in life, as it's your responsibility to be so. "You are complete within yourself, Megha," he told her.

*Love doesn't compete with or complete you. It complements you.*

This became the new mantra in Megha's life, as she kept on repeating those words to herself all time, believing in the power of affirmations, as the coach had guided her.

She knew she was worthy of love, who isn't ?

But a nagging voice still haunted in the back of her mind, one that continuously warned her that she wasn't deserving of the kind of love she had always dreamt for, the kind of love in the movies, so gentle, kind, passionate, and full of positivity.

Her life had changed so much in such a short span.

While she had stopped waiting for the perfect man to come and fulfil her dreams, even as she rebuilt herself, Megha couldn't avoid the burning yet passive desire to be loved, not in spite of her past trauma, but because of it.

Continuing her journey of self-love, Megha decided to go on a backpacker's trip with a bunch of people from her city she found online, headed by an experienced travel enthusiast. Clueless how it was going to be, she felt letting herself lose in the mystery of uncertainty, to spread her wings and cherish whatever was about to come her way.

After all, when we can trust the pilot of our flight or the train driver, why can't we allow the universe to guide us, manoeuvre our next moves when we are confused, wondering what to do next in our lives.

Megha was set to sail with the winds…

It was a Saturday afternoon when they left for the trip.

It was the first time she connected with strangers since her break-up, feeling happy with her new approach to life. She loved this vibe, quiet, cozy and perfect for escaping the world for a while.

As she sat at the window in the bus, sipping on her latte, flipping through the pages of a book, she went down the memory lane, again. But this time, it wasn't the sad, odd experience she remembered, instead, she recollected her lovely and lively nature, which used to light up every space she entered, not merely in social gatherings, but the darkest of spaces in anyone's heart.

Megha was back; back to the future !

Megha, are you there? She heard someone saying, wondering who's calling her in the bus full of unknown people, who weren't introduced to each other yet. It was the tour guide, the one heading their trip, counting heads, ensuring everyone who'd signed up had boarded the trip.

"Yes, I'm in," confirmed Megha, as she looked at this guy, ready to take them all on their four days trip, a journey of their lifetime. Nobody knew much about the surprises planned for them (as mentioned in the trip brochure). Still, everyone was so excited to see what came up next.

Isn't it quite thrilling to explore the unexplored, know the unknown, see the unseen; that's what life is all about…

Megha couldn't help but notice the gentle way Aayush acknowledged everyone's presence in the bus, making everyone feel warmly welcomed on the trip. There was something about him that made her feel drawn to him. While she was continuously staring at him as he made certain announcements, she quickly looked back down at her book, when he made an eye contact with her. But the curiosity to glance at him again lingered in her mind.

"Hi, welcome aboard once again, I'm going to be your support for our four days excursion", said Aayush, extending his hand towards Megha, with a smile on his face and confidence in his eyes.

She felt an unexpected jolt, a shiver ran down her spine, as he came and sat down next to her, with a genuine smile, directly touching her soul.

"I couldn't help but notice your book. Not sure if I've read it too. Are you liking it?" asked Aayush.

Taken aback by his words, Megha looked at him from the side, with the sunlight shining on his face across the window. She had always been more of an observer, someone who won't randomly connect with strangers. But Aayush's calm demeanor made her feel at ease.

"It's an interesting read," she said, keeping her book aside, hinting at her willingness and excitement to carry on this conversation with him.

Who would like to read a book at this moment, isn't it ?

Aayush smiled at her again, with eyes twinkling, replied, "I agree. It's a book that stays with you long after you've finished it." Not sure what he was hinting at though.

While he had to attend other guests onboard as well, he would return, sit next to Megha and their journey continued. They spent some time chatting about the book she was reading earlier, exchanging their views about the plot, how the story evolved and emotions flowed.

The conversation continued effortlessly, as Megha felt a warmth she hadn't experienced in a long time. It was neither flirtatious nor a forced one, but a sweet, normal chit-chat two people carried on about everything they loved, and it felt so real. From school to college and beyond, every topic was touched upon in this heart-to-heart exchange, sharing similar places of interest in their city, from the famous *paani-puri* hawker to *chai wala* stall, next to old railway station. Belonging to the same city and frequented such common eateries or so, they'd never met earlier, yet found so much in common to gossip about.

Nonetheless, the alarm rang in her mind and she couldn't help but feel a little cautious. She had been hurt before, twice, a connection which started in a similar way but got disconnected, leaving her soul torn behind.

How could she throw herself into the circle of love, without being certain of Aayush's intentions? There's no guarantee in love, a lesson she had learnt the hard way…

As the bus went through twists and turns on the road uphill, Megha's mind went through a roller coaster ride, lost inside, while still carrying on the chat with him.

Aayush must have noticed her being uneasy, as he leaned back, giving her a reassuring smile, said in a low voice "Life is not meant to rush every time, instead, take a pause, reflect on what you really want, and then take an appropriate action." It seemed like he wasn't just a tour guide, but a mind reader, who could travel through her heart, mind and soul, knowing it all.

Megha surprised by his deep insight, replied, "I didn't really get it what you meant."

"It's alright Megha, everything is not meant to be understood immediately. It's absolutely fine to take your time, which is a good thing. Being impatient won't get us anything real. I respect that."

Oh my goodness ! What did he just say?

His words astonished Megha way more than she expected. More than mere words, the way he said it with such simplicity, reflected the understanding she always wanted. Something always unnoticed within her felt recognized. She felt the urge to tell him everything that had happened in her past, but she kept quiet, pondering whether she should so soon.

While the bus reached its final stop, their exchange of feelings had just started.

The next morning arrived quite afresh, full of adventure, meeting new people in the group, sharing a hearty breakfast after a long trek, soaking up the sun all along.

Aayush was around, taking care of everyone personally, more than the arrangements, displaying his natural social skills, making everyone feel comfortable and relaxed in new surroundings, similar to what Megha felt with him in the bus last evening.

On their way back, she slipped on a turn and Aayush came to her rescue, giving more than just first aid.

"You know what, I've been hurt before," Megha said, while Aayush held her swollen foot in his hand. "Honestly, I wonder if I'll trust someone again."

Aayush didn't respond, just gave a nod. After administering basic first aid, she was able to walk with a limp, holding his hand, all the way down to the base camp.

"I get it Megha," he said, in a soft yet firm voice, as he made her lie down gently in her bed. "In fact, I won't like you to jump into anything too early dear, unless you're standing firm on your feet," he implied more than her physical hurt, as he knew what a girl wants.

He went on describing his idea about relationships, sounding quite mature and responsible in the matters of the heart, knowing what it really meant to promise in love – until death do us apart…

Megha felt something different about Aayush's words, unlike whatever she had heard in her past. Neither he was promising nor seeking any perfection, but offering a possibility for both to live life together, a real connection.

"I can't rush into anything, I just don't want to yet, but I'd definitely like to know if you're serious, as I won't be able to take the pain of heartbreak, again" Megha said.

"Trust I won't lie to you, I'm not here to play with your heart, but take it away. You have my word and you will always remember this night, if you wish to walk the path."

Here it came – the real promise, from a man of words.

It wasn't a promise to woo a girl and take her advantage, but an earnest attempt to build a connection, an assurance that this could be the beginning of something real yet magical, something worth waiting for all these years.

"I'm not asking anything from you right now, except an opportunity to prove that I'm the one you can trust," Aayush continued.

Megha loved everything he spoke, straight from his heart. But she didn't say anything, rather asked him to switch off the light, pretending to be sleepy, while still in real pain.

Whenever in doubt, sleep over it, her coach said once.

She wanted her subconscious mind to guide, assist in making up her mind – whether she must say Yes or No !

Megha woke up early next morning, third day of their trip, stepped out of her bed, paused for a moment, feeling a mix of emotions inside, and rushed to Aayush's room.

Her coach's idea worked like magic. She had found her answer. No, she wasn't going to say those 3 magical words immediately, but the hope and belief that this was the kind of love she awaited all her life, was finally there.

"I think I'd like to see you win my trust someday," Megha said hurriedly, as Aayush opened the door. There was an expression of fear and vulnerability in her eyes though.

Aayush held her hand, placed it on his heart, smiled and said, "Leave your worries to me, my dear. I'll take care." While his words were so reassuring, a sudden flash of memory dimmed her eyes, as she recalled how Aryan had proposed her with such comforting words.

But this time, she didn't let her past rule her present, as this wasn't a rushed decision, but a well thought over move in the right direction, a leap of faith, a gift of nature.

As they exchanged numbers on their return next day, Megha felt excited and agreed to meet him again, soon. Neither a fairy tale nor love at first sight. Certainly not a movie directed by Bollywood but a true story, yet to begin, with real-life characters, determined to walk the talk, with

*The Real Promise…*

# 6. Cuddles & Caress :)

Change, the Only Constant thing in the world, was quite evident in Megha's life, all gratitude to Aayush's presence, her coach's guidance and of course her own courage to conquer her fear.

After the memorable trip, Megha restructured her professional life. After a long break from work, she got placed in a new role, with higher rewards and responsibilities, and a renewed sense of energy to outperform her peers.

"I got it, thank you so much," read Megha's message, leaving Aayush confused what was she talking about, in her first ever message she sent, after coming back from the trip. Aayush hadn't text her anything until now, as he wanted to give her time to feel more relaxed and comfortable enough to initiate the conversation.

He was quite certain she will get back to him, soon…

"I'm really glad to know you got whatever you wished, Megha. Let's catch up to know more about it and celebrate your win" Aayush typed but then, just deleted it.

He didn't want to sound desperate to meet her, as he wasn't either. He knew pretty well that his relationship with Megha was going to cook well only on a low flame, and any sign of rushing through will burn all to ashes.

So, all he replied was, "Awesome Megha, that's so cool, so happy for you."

His patience and understanding were rewarded with something unexpected, as Megha replied, "Hey, it's something I wanna share with you. Let's meet today?"

Nothing fancy but a small café was the venue for their first ever catch up after the trip. It was a renowned one though, famous for its hot coffee and delectable cheese sandwiches, a perfect place for melting hearts and coming together as one.

Being punctual, yet another admirable quality he had, Aayush was there sharp at 7, waiting with curiosity, wondering what did Megha have to say.

And then, the café's door opened, with dangling bells ringing, as Megha entered, wearing a long, shining dress, eyes glowing with all the happiness to see him again. He stood up to receive her, like a true gentleman, pulling her chair and making her seated comfortably, in this cosy café, full of warmth and aroma.

"I was skeptical if I could make it after such a long haul, still I tried, and guess what, I got it, a big break in one of the industry's top player, as a senior consultant ! OMG ! Trust, I still can't believe myself it happened Aayush," Megha was almost in tears, as she shared the big news.

*When a woman is extremely happy, she cries…*

But she won't express her emotions in front of everyone; vulnerability is a gift she won't share with everybody.

Well, Megha's release of pent-up emotions in front of Aayush assured of one thing to both – this association was meant for something fruitful in future.

And they continued enjoying this moment, as he picked up a chocolate cake to celebrate her victory, full of sweetness in real sense, unlike the dark chocolate.

The weeks that followed were full of small moments that added up to something bigger than what Megha thought. Small and sweet exchange of texts throughout the day, those long telephonic conversations late night, whispering sweet little voice notes while in office, it was a time full of something that wasn't love, at least not in the sense everyone thinks it is, no grand gestures, but something quiet, full of comfort and peace, something more profound, allowing both to be themselves as they were.

It was the beginning of a slow and steady connection, which had the potential to flourish beyond measure.

In this world full of varied experiences, Aayush had almost become a constant in her life, her go-to person in every situation or someone to share everything first.

While she was welcoming every moment with open arms, they weren't overwhelming in any way that love could have made her feel otherwise. She knew where she was and what were both looking forward to in the present, without worrying what's coming up in their future.

Love or any relationship is supposed to be a supportive and soothing affair, full of trust and care; not meant to create a heavy feeling or burden on one's mind.

The episodes directed by M&A (Megha & Aayush) productions were like a rom-com, unlike what led to a split in an erstwhile M&A (Megha & Aryan) association.

There were neither dramatic nor lovey-dovey moments, or rushed decisions how they would define their bond, and most important, no pressure on either side to reach to any conclusions.

Just two people, sailing with the currents, tuning into each other's frequency, adapting themselves to the space they occupied in each other's lives. Megha was taking it slow this time, the way she never believed would happen, unlike her past, impulsive encounters in love.

But this time, it was different, a smooth sailing with Aayush, grounded enough for it to thrive.

They started meeting quite frequently, almost every weekend now, catching up for movie or a casual dinner at some famous place. Other times, it was an impromptu tea-talk at the *chai wala* stall, next to old railway station.

Megha found herself laughing naturally around him, something that seemed rare in her life after the devastation she'd been through. She was opening up like the rose bud, so delicately, taking time, letting every moment seep in so slow, like the winter morning dew.

Why not?

She was being so well received by the keeper of her emotions, the guardian of her heart, the saviour of her life, Aayush, who used to look at her with such kindness and openness, as if seeing through the core of her heart.

He seemed to be a pro in handling a broken heart, helping her overcome past hurt in love, which requires tremendous amount of patience, empathy and unwavering support.

The first thing Aayush provided Megha with was a safe space, where she would feel encouraged to speak her heart and share her feelings, without being judged.

He would provide her an active listening ear, allowing her to take as much time she wanted to vent out her pain, while validating her emotions and comforting her that it's okay to feel hurt. He knew healing takes time, and now, she also believed he was with her, patiently and willingly.

Her belief about him wasn't built overnight !

He was consistent, his words and actions matched, and his behavior demonstrated loyalty and transparency, paving the foundation for rebuilding trust in her heart.

He would give her all possible time and attention, something a girl wants most, along with respect, which Megha also had for Aayush.

After all, he earned it by encouraging Megha to focus on self-love, self-care, self-confidence & sense of self-worth.

He became her biggest cheer-leader, always reminding her of her strengths, holding her every time she would dwell in the past, never making her feel bad about whatever wrong choices she made, but always pulling her back into who she really was and the love she deserves.

Healing from past hurt can never be instantaneous, and it's crucial to avoid rushing the process, as it's a journey, a series of steps one needs to take, before moving on to the other side for good.

Aayush was there with Megha, seamlessly providing his unconditional support throughout, while letting her know that there was a bright future possible for her, together, so when trust becomes deep rooted, like a bedrock of inevitable strength, love would flourish and the rose petals would bloom in all its glory.

Any girl would go gaga over a guy like him, isn't it?

But despite all his efforts, Megha could still feel occasional bout of doubt inside her. It wasn't that she doubted Aayush but she didn't trust herself, her decision making, whether she could really open her heart again, allow someone to occupy a special space therein, even when it had been invaded before, leaving behind a fragmented heart? Could she expose herself just for the sake of love?

Megha was stuck at the crossroads, unable to make an informed choice, which way to steer her life, whether she could choose to propose or accept it from Aayush.

Aayush, the patient guy, avoided pushing her. He never asked for anything from her. He was just around her. Time and again, he showed up whenever needed most.

Eventually, Megha let go of her fears and inhibition, as she understood that we get life just once, and there's no room for unhappiness, so she can't let her present and future destroyed at the cost of her past, which is over. There is no harm in letting herself free from the miseries she was clouded with, so new drops of fresh spell of love could drizzle on her face and touch her soul deep inside.

So, now she was certain that if he is meant to be, so be it. She was okay to go with the flow and see where this union will lead to, whether they will fall in love or not, will it remain just an extraordinary friendship or something else.

Megha just wanted to let nothing come in between her and the bright future ahead. She was fully optimistic now.

One fine morning, Aayush met Megha right outside her office, as she was about to step inside the building, and invited her over to his apartment for a dinner, giving her full freedom to decide all day long, if she was okay or not, reassuring her that neither he would mind nor she had to give any explanations, if she chose not to come.

But he kept waiting until evening, with something quite thoughtful and special arrangements made for her – homemade pasta cooked by himself, paired with a bottle of champagne, the typical one Megha had mentioned once on their trip, and hot chocolate brownie to drool over.

Will she come or not, he wasn't sure, as there was no message or call from Megha all day, and he purposely avoided too. Aayush never wanted to sound overbearing but kept his fingers crossed.

Suddenly the bell rang and his heart sank, but, just like Aayush, you guessed it wrong too. It wasn't Megha, but a florist to deliver a huge bouquet of mixed roses. There was also a small greeting card attached to it, which read – "I'm sorry Aayush, but I won't be able to make it. I don't know what to say, except that I understand you will definitely feel bad. But I'm helpless, you know. Neither I'm able to leave things behind, nor I want to stop myself from moving ahead, hence I'm stuck somewhere in the middle, clueless what to do with my life. I know you've waited long enough, but I don't want to test your patience. – Megha"

Sad and disappointed, he sat down on the floor, right next to the door, when he heard the same delivery boy, knocking the door and saying, "Sir, there's something more left here, which I forgot to deliver."

Aayush got up, disheartened, to open the door and to his surprise, there was Megha, standing next to the delivery boy, with an almond chocolate (his favourite) in her hand, smiling and saying, "this is what he missed I guess."

Megha, the bubbly-girl alive, wanted to surprise Aayush with this small prank. In fact, she got this bouquet of roses delivered from the same florist stall, she came across once in a mall, when she was recovering from her situationship.

While Aayush was still recovering from the shocking surprise she gave him that evening, Megha was touched with the special arrangements for her, feeling at ease, with the soft lighting and music playing in the background.

The table was set for two, a candle light delight, she was about to take pleasure in, with a touch of his calmness in the romantic set up.

"Hey, this looks too good," she said, her voice full of genuine appreciation, as they sat down at the table, and he gifted her an antique make-up box.

"It's nothing better than what you brought for me today – yourself, oh Megha ! You're the best gift I ever received," said Aayush, in his loving voice, with the candle flickering, in the stillness of their breath…

This was the magic spell Aayush casted on Megha, always.

In that moment, Megha realized that this was real love, that she could let flow in her life. No extravagant affairs but small moments spent together, the sumptuous homemade meals, the laughter over silly jokes, the quiet and genuine conversations while sipping champagne or *chai*, and everything in between.

After dinner, they settled onto the couch. Megha, while leaning against Aayush and her head resting on his shoulder, realized how much she had started trusting him, loving his patience wrapped with authenticity, a rare diamond-like quality.

It felt so easy and obvious, something like they had experienced countless times before. Aayush wrapped his arm around her gently, and the soft teddy bear inside her was drawn closer towards him. A warm embrace, melting her heart, in a moment of intimacy, she never felt before.

Megha raised her head slightly, looking into his eyes and asked, "Are we doing it right Aayush? I hope we're not rushing into anything."

"I'm sure whatever we are feeling right now is natural. Nothing planned or felt earlier, I suppose, isn't it, Megha? If it wasn't right for you, you would have never been here today. You've come a long way, at your free will. Now, let nothing stop you from experiencing you always wanted. Remember, you're in safe hands, Megha."

All she wanted was such kind of assurance from a man, who wasn't with her merely for physical pursuits, but earnestly willing to create an emotional bond, inevitable for a girl before giving in herself fully.

Megha closed her eyes, while resting in his arms, allowing herself to feel those words of comfort, settle deep within. Aayush was the anchor her restless mind always needed. He was steady and calm, gifting her with time and space to breathe again, heal and finally trust someone in love.

"I'd never imagined letting someone knock at my heart again, but with you, it doesn't feel like I have to be afraid."

Aayush, cuddling her softly, "You don't need to worry, Megha. I'm always there for you, with all my sincerity, imperfection and willingness to just be yours. I'm what you see me right now, with all my flaws and vulnerability, and all I'm looking for is someone real, just like you."

Real, oh yes ! All she was yearning for – something real. Not some idealized version but real form of love, ingrained with mutual respect and understanding, built on the foundation of trust, acknowledging imperfections, while offering unconditional support to each other.

A deep sense of security prevailed. She didn't have to pretend to be someone she wasn't or feel something odd about being natural, she had enough of it with Aryan.

She could just be Megha…

"Thank you for everything you've done for me so patiently, for giving me time and space, letting me heal and being myself, handling my ups and downs, and still being there for me, always," said Megha, hugging him so tight.

"Of course, Megha. That's what true love is all about, isn't it? Being there for each other, and showing up every time, especially when things get ugly," Aayush whispered in her ears, as she rested her face, so close to his cheeks.

The evening continued, with M&A wrapped up in their arms, nestled in the warmth their presence brought for each other, with Aayush resting lightly on her shoulder, and Megha getting closer, rejoicing the kind of love she always wanted.

With Aayush by her side, Megha finally allowed herself to ride the high tide of love, that wouldn't just endure the test of time but foster a soulful, sensual connection full of

*Cuddles & Caress :)*

# 7.  Kiss of Love…

"A night to remember…

This is how I'd cherish this moment together, for the years to come," said Megha, with her eyes still closed, lost like *Alice in Wonderland.*

She seemed lost in her dreams, while feeling sleepy in his arms, a cushion of comfort and care, just like any girl would feel so calm and relaxed, with the man she loves.

"I love you, now I'm sure I do, to the moon and back," Megha's voice full of devotion, for the man in her life.

The real promise, they exchanged that night, a vow made unanimously, to 'gift themselves' to each other, forever, as a gift is an expression of immense significance our partner holds in the relationship. When we choose a gift for someone special, we ensure to be mindful of their likes and dislikes, with a feeling of empathy and gratitude.

The perfect gift, both received, crafted with love…

Love was no more a complicated notion for Megha.

While her early experiences were quite unjustified, this new affair was just and fair. In such times of fast food, their love had simmered over the slow flame, ignited with love and fuelled with patience and perseverance.

They had time-travelled together, managing different stages of relationship so meticulously.

After meeting Aayush for the first time during the trip, she developed an unknown crush and felt excited about the possibility of a new beginning, while feeling awkward and nervousness about the dynamics.

All this while and after coming home, he was always on her mind, flashing through her thoughts all day and night, during the honeymoon phase.

Moving into the period of uncertainty, she was nonplussed at Aayush's expressions of certainty, yet uncertain, whether or not this relation was built to last.

And finally, as she decided to hang in there, in a respectfully carved out mutual partnership, she realised how smooth this sailing was, across the stages, with the relentless support of such a partner, found so rare in life.

Their relationship had progressed in ways nobody could ever imagine. Being sceptical of love, especially after whatever she went through, they had come quite far, and it was worth it.

It was time to enter the new season…

A thing which doesn't grow, dies !

They had spent months together, their bond growing with time. While a relationship needs continuous effort to thrive, the easy comfort built together now evolved into something running on autopilot mode, that Megha had always thought impossible.

She remembered what Myra said once during her visit, and called her to narrate her story with Aayush.

Myra was so overjoyed to hear that Megha had finally triumphed in life, her wounds healed, void filled with someone's pure love, who's hand she could hold confidently and trust him blindly to follow his footsteps, unafraid of the consequences anymore.

Myra loved teasing Megha about her first visit to Aayush's apartment, eager to know how was the night spent between the two lovebirds.

"Well, it was nothing as you're daydreaming Myra, nothing unusual or special, just two of us being close enough to feel each other's heartbeat, hear those unspoken words, in a pin drop silence, that's it," Megha described.

*Kiss of Love, Kiss of Love, Stay Away from Kiss of Love...*

Myra sang this peppy song from a musical rom-com Bollywood movie, *Jhoom Barabar Jhoom*, pulling Megha's leg, how could anyone stay away from the kiss of love?

"You're crazy Myra, bbye..." Megha hung up the phone.

Next day was Aayush's birthday and he invited Megha to his apartment, along with his other set of friends. Megha couldn't sleep the previous night, as she was super excited to 'meet and greet' him on his special day, after wishing him at twelve o'clock at night. It was his first birthday they would celebrate after being in their relationship.

"You're looking so happy after so long my child," said Megha's mother, as she was about to leave for her office.

"Yes Mumma, it's Aayush's birthday today, and we are celebrating it tonight at his place, where he's going to introduce me to his friends, oh I'm so excited, Cya." Megha rushed in excitement, barely able to concentrate at work, counting every minute for the long day to pass, and stars to shine, to hug him so tight, under the moonlight.

She left early from office that day, as she had to buy him a gift, besides something special she had planned already.

After checking out lots of options at different stores in a nearby mall, she stood still for a while, and asked herself - What could be the best gift to match a classy person like Aayush? What's that utmost special thing he's done, which needs to be recognised in the most glorified yet humble manner, that would bring a big smile on his face?

Something clicked her mind, and she rushed to the famous store on the ground floor, to buy something for the most uplifting yet so grounded man in her life.

All the way, while driving, she just hoped that he likes it…

When Megha walked into Aayush's apartment, she was greeted with a warm welcome surprise by all his friends, as confetti showered upon her from the ceiling.

Aayush had already announced Megha's special arrival to her friends, who greeted her so lovingly, as if they knew each other since ages. Seemed like it was her birthday !

They had a cheerful conversation while enjoying the flavoursome food with wine pouring, and everyone dancing to the tunes of their favourite numbers. It was a gala occasion, with special performances by all his dear friends, followed by the couple dance by the two soulmates, just before everyone left, while Megha stayed.

While Aayush locked the door, Megha seated herself in the couch, ready with the lovely gifts she had got for him. When he came close, sitting next to her, she kept looking into her eyes, silently soaking in the calmness on his face.

"Aayush, you gave me the most invaluable thing in this world, 'your time', time to heal, time to understand myself, my identity, what I really want in life, time to get over everything I went through. You've been so patient in loving and caring, letting me being myself, a gift I can never reciprocate.

Still, I'd like to give you something, nowhere close to what you've done for me though; this classic piece of watch for the class-apart personality like you, who deserves nothing but the best. I'm giving you this watch as a symbol of my firm commitment, to be yours this lifetime, oh my love," said Megha, as tears rolled down her cheeks.

"There's something more I got for you, Aayush," said Megha, as she pulled out a hand-knitted sweater for him. "It was quite fun to see my grandma doing tick-tick with those chopsticks-like needles, so I learnt how to make these designs in my teenage. I'd love to see you wearing this, feeling the warmth of our embrace," she continued.

Aayush was really touched at this point with Megha's words dipped in love. Her innocent admiration and fondness for Aayush, ticking every second in that classic watch, and the soft and bright, designer red sweater, knitted with love – *what a birthday gift for Aayush…*

Something felt different tonight, a shift between the two, a surge of emotions, a new energy in the room, something unusual blooming, with love in the air, creating an undeniable charge between them, an undercurrent of deeper sentiments coming to the surface, more of an intimacy, than mere companionship they had developed, as they were absorbed inside each other's eyes.

They didn't talk anything at this moment, as silence spoke louder, and eyes could read the imprints on their heart. Megha couldn't resist being so close to him now, in these tender moments, building up with every breath, as she felt it so natural to be so close to him, and her mind, body and soul so keen to lean into him, without any resistance.

She wasn't someone to fall in love so easily after past hurt, or experience the kind of proximity where two hearts beat together as one in complete synchrony. But with Aayush, everything felt like a complete picture.

Aayush held Megha's left hand with his right, with a soft, feather-like gentle but deliberate touch, fingers intertwined, as if trying to write something in her palm. His left hand was behind her shoulder, gently caressing, playful around her curly hair, pulling her gently so closer, with barely any space left.

Megha, with her heart racing, didn't push him away, as he leaned even further, glancing into her beautiful eyes, full of meaning. With his warm breath across her face, his lips resting almost just above her lips, in a sensational encounter, so electrifying. With a deep, slow breath, she just closed her eyes, with a pounding heartbeat.

And then, in this perfect setting, Aayush kissed Megha.

The moment their lips met, something happened deep inside her, a sense of euphoria, a magical experience, which invoked varied emotions, taking her on cloud nine. For the first time in years, she felt safe and alive, again, while the kiss of love still leaving her breathless.

"All fine? You, okay?" he asked gently, as they pulled away, smiling and reviving together from a fictional ride, like a dream come true.

Megha nodded in affirmation, still short of words to explain what she felt. Her heart still pumping really fast, her mind clueless, lost in paradise, but all she could focus on was the kiss of love, Aayush had brought in her life — *what a return gift for Megha…*

"I think it's more than just fine," she whispered finally, her voice still recovering from the heavy emotions she felt. "I think it's exactly what I needed ever since we met. I just took a lot of time but it's worth it," she continued.

"When you kissed me, it felt as if the world around us had disappeared. Everything inside me just melted away, as all I could focus on was you, my love. I wasn't prepared for how it would impact me; how would I feel doing so with you, but it was so comforting in the way you kissed me, it made the entire experience so gentle and so full of feeling.

The way your lips hovered upon mine, resting so soft in the beginning, and diving further, while we discovered something deep about us, made me feel something can't be described in words. A craving full of curiosity, an openness without fear, a journey to our final destination."

Megha kept going with so much love, to speak her heart…

*"Sitting next to you upright, it just felt so right, when you held me so close and tight, in the moment so passionate yet light, eyes closed but future seemed bright, darkness wiped off with light, our love rising to another height, an experience so delight, your lips so warm to ignite, intimate episodes in this special night."*

After all, this kiss was really so special; it wasn't neither forced nor filled with any sort of urgency or hurry, in fact, it was soft, tender, sweet, and an inviting affair for Megha, which she loved to match equally, by pulling him around, kissing him back once more.

As they grew closer, the anticipation of what was coming up now, sent a shiver down her spine, awaiting the evolution of the next phase in their relationship.

While she continued surfing through his lips, he gently cupped her face, his thumbs sliding along her cheekbones, feeling the softness of her skin.

When their bodies finally aligned, Megha felt a subtle mix of emotions. Beyond those physical sensations, what she felt was a profound sense of emotional connection. There was no rush or anxiety, as every touch, every move was slow, both savouring the moment, which wasn't just a physical connection, but a deeper layer of intimacy.

As they continued their sensual exploration, they rolled down on the floor, rediscovering each other, in all those forbidden spaces; Aayush wrapping her firm in his arms, as if she was his most priceless possession.

The soft, rhythmic motion of their bodies invited them even closer, their movements more in sync, dancing like ballet, as they shared a soul-stirring connection they had just started to explore. There was a certain gentleness in their wilderness, an unsaid assurance that they were in this together, willingly, lost yet fully present in the moment.

Every touch, the shared warmth and breathlessness, spoke volumes about the bond, like it was meant to be.

As they pulled apart, with faces still close and eyes locked, holding around in tranquillity, ushering into a new world.

Megha felt her thoughts beginning to settle now.

While she believed that intimacy should be a reflection of emotional indulgence, but experiencing it in real terms with someone she fully trusted was a different feeling altogether. It was an acceptance in her entirety, a respect for mutual needs and boundaries.

What outshined for her in those moments wasn't just the physical connect, though she loved the ride, but it was the depth of emotions they touched. She realized that she was with the most sorted person in love, someone who desired her more than her body, someone who knew pretty well how to pull her heartstrings, think through her thoughts, help fight with her fears, value her in every aspect.

Megha also found deeply connected to herself in that moment, while they shared their vulnerability together.

The sense of freedom this emotional and physical closeness gifted her was quite liberating. She didn't have to model anybody's world or worry about her looks or perception anymore, as she was being what she would simply love to – the real Megha.

When this moment passed; more than just a fleeting physical release, it was the quiet understanding and reflection of something much deeper, that had formed the foundation of their relationship. She felt safe, loved and deeply connected, a feeling that stayed with her long after the physical moment had passed.

Later that night, as they sipped hot chocolate together in the warmth of the living room, they realised that there was something sacred about their relationship, which wasn't rushed or had any selfish interests. It was rather coming from the place of willingness to give, more and more, holding each other like a blindfold dance between two people, who had chosen to trust each other completely, not out of desperation or insecurity, but sheer love.

A love that was unconditional, rare and deeply powerful, which existed without any conditions. It was constant, regardless of one's past or present situations. It wasn't seeking any perfection or reciprocity, instead looked forward to gift acceptance and unwavering support.

Aayush's love remained constant for Megha, even during her difficult times, when she seemed messed up, and their relationship wasn't mature. Still, he kept loving her for who she was, irrespective of how she felt about him, as the best thing he knew in life was how to give love effortlessly.

How could Megha be left behind in reciprocating him with all that he truly deserved in love. A pure soul like Megha could duly recognise his sincerity in love, his humanity in forgiving her imperfections, and staying devoted to her, even before actually being committed in the relationship, through all its ups and downs.

Such was the premise of their love, ensuring deep, loving and forever lasting connections.

"Hey Megha," he whispered, in a voice full of emotions, "I want you to know that I'm here with you, for the rest of my life, as long you would like to be around at least."

His words, full of meaning and sincerity, felt so soothing. She had heard him saying so earlier too, but this time, it felt different, like a promise, more than just words, which guaranteed a future, no matter how uncertain it seemed.

"I'm here too with you," replied Megha, holding his hand. "I'm ready for whatever follows in our life, together."

Whatever happened that night wasn't a chance encounter, rather destined, blessing the duo with all that was so meant for such lovebirds.

Her manifestation came true, emancipating her from the limiting beliefs, Megha had developed about herself, as a new love was born tonight, with Aayush by her side, holding their future together, lip locked in their passionate

*Kiss of Love…*

# 8. Love : Virus or Vaccine?

The first light of dawn peeping through the red curtains, spread a soft ambient light across the room. Megha lay beside Aayush, the love of her life, with a comfort she cherished in his arms.

As she looked at Aayush's sleeping face, she started to notice his features more closely, tapping her fingers like playing a piano on his cheeks. His sharp, well-defined jawline, a reflection of his confidence and masculinity, which handled her feminine energy so well. His clear skin was a mirror image of his kind and compassionate nature, making him so desirable for Megha.

Love had found its way, piercing through the inaccessible walls she had built around her heart, redefining her personality and mindset about what love is; and she could feel the change, ever since she met him, evolved into Megha 2.0

This evolution wasn't a cakewalk but fire walk for Megha, as she witnessed different variants of love in her lifetime.

Every relationship she entered was painted with different colors of love, brushed with unique strokes by every artist, sweeping her heart away, with fifty shades of grey.

Understanding these different types of love was crucial for her personal growth, as such experiences weaving through her life helped to figure out what she really needed in life & relationships and what she was willing to offer to her partner in such mutual exchange.

It's vital to remember that no two relationships are same, even for the same individual experiencing it, as the way they express or feel love with someone is as diverse as their partners' personality.

Reflecting on the types of love present in one's life helps us identify which ones dominate or seem dormant, giving clarity on what seems fulfilling or lacking in real terms. Love isn't a one-size-fits-all experience, it can never be, and that's what makes it so personal.

Living through such ups and downs in life form the foundation of our meaningful connections developed over time, with each form of love playing its own role in defining how we reflect on our inner-self and forge alliances with people around us.

Megha learnt these major lessons of life, the hard way…

Infatuation, an intense crush, was her first ever experience in the realms of love.

The overwhelming feeling, where she couldn't stop thinking about that guy, with heightened emotions and the excitement of the unknown, quite thrilling, was short-lived. Megha wasn't merely sunk in this type of fantasy, she was actually drowned. She didn't just skip her heartbeat, but had a heart attack, when reality bite. Her dreams and reality were shaken, when this situationship fizzled out so soon.

The second encounter in her life was far away from love, an obsession, where desires became unhealthy.

While it started with something bright, the feelings of intense passion, it quickly went down the dark lane, darker than one's own shadow, where she couldn't recognize herself anymore, as she was under the negative influence and control of Aryan, who just wanted to have her possession, without giving her space to breathe, trapped in a suffocating cage of so-called love.

There was no mutual respect or partnership, instead, it was all about her emotional manipulation and mental hijack, as she lost her ability to function independently.

What seemed like love with Aryan, had crossed its line into obsession, emotionally damaging to her, lacking those healthy boundaries and mutual growth, something that could truly define a loving relationship.

In fact, what Aryan gave Megha was one of the most painful forms of love, where her genuine, deep feelings were never reciprocated in real. All that she felt in the start was a mere eyewash.

This unrequited love kept her waiting hopelessly in the dark tunnel, with no light or end in sight. The pain of its imbalance, where she kept investing herself emotionally, with Aryan being indifferent, unwilling and unable to payback her love, something which even money can't buy. It was a disbalanced see-saw ride in the park of love, where he was enjoying up in the air, weighing down heavily upon the feelings of a light hearted, heart-rending teddy inside her.

This series of deceit lead to a spiral of unwanted feelings inside her mind, and she started questioning her self-worth, considering herself inadequate for Aryan. The self-doubt seeped through the layers of her heart faster than blood, as her soul was fired with bullets of rejection.

Despite all she could, her efforts never bore fruit, in this meaningless love, which never had a happy ending.

But unrequited love left behind the great learnings about resilience, the ability to cope and recover from setbacks, soothing oneself patiently, with the balm of self-love.

We can't force someone to love us the way we do, Megha concluded, as she let go of Aryan and moved on, rising in a new dawn with Aayush.

Love had always been a challenging concept for Megha, something scary, leaving her feeling empty from within. Her experiences made her believe that love was a virus – an insidious force that spread and eventually destroyed.

*Love, is it really a virus?*

Ah well, when love happens with the wrong person, it can begin to emerge like a harmful virus, infecting every part of one's emotional and mental well-being, leading to a huge negative impact on one's physical health too. Just like virus attacks every cell of our body, toxic love can seep into our heart and mind, causing utter chaos in life.

When symptoms of an illness are barely noticeable in its early stages, a relationship with the wrong person may feel exciting, as our mind is clouded with the mist of love.

However, with the passage of time, the darker aspects of such relationship begin to emerge, when the rose seems to have lost its fragrance, the artificial sweetness of the chocolate tastes bitter, words begin to lie, as the virus of manipulation and control begins to multiply.

The immunity of the heart starts weakening with every instance of gaslighting, and the illusion of fake love kills the perception of reality, one has about themselves, causing instability and confusion, created by deception, where the victim feels trapped in a cycle of mistrust and emotional turmoil, caused by the parasite in love.

The toxic virus causes lack of real, meaningful connection in such relations, draining life out of the one suffering. The connection lacks genuine emotional intimacy and is merely driven by bodily desires, making one feel used.

As it becomes more poisonous, this association becomes a breeding ground for insecurities and anger, often attacking the other with spiteful words, out of hatred.

Like a mutating virus, such exploitation surge over time.

Just like a virus is too small to be seen with an optical microscope, impossible to be visible with a human eye, it can be extremely difficult to eradicate, leaving long lasting impact on the immune system. So is the damage caused by a destructive relationship can stay long after it ends. The emotional disfigurement takes a lot of time to heal, leaving the wounded with the aftermath of a crime, nowhere yet defined in any court of law.

Ultimately, an abusive or negative relationship with a wrong person is so detrimental to one's ability to trust, love, and build healthy relationships in the future.

A poisonous relationship like virus, spreads negativity and harm, eroding the emotional landscape and individuality. A strong reminder of the necessity of choosing the right partner, recognizing early signs of negativity and protecting oneself from dysfunctional relationships.

*From the point of view of someone destroyed in love, it's a virus!*

Things had changed for Megha; she felt alive, inside out.

Aayush had gifted her with a bouquet of varied experiences in personal life, beginning with selfless love, putting her first, always.

His love was all about giving without expecting anything in return, when her well-being and happiness was always prioritized, beautifully expressed through his willingness to understand, continuous acts of sacrifice and support, coming from a place of genuine care and concern.

He was never controlling or seeking any validation, his love completely free from ego. Not merely unconditional, he wasn't even looking for any recognition, being driven by the desire to make her life better.

Since he loved her without malice intentions, it helped her start trusting someone again in life, as she developed unshaken faith in him. It isn't that she hadn't trusted men in her previous relations, but, as they say, you can't clap with one hand alone; it takes two to tango.

This mindset allowed both to receive happiness in love.

Enduring love, that lasts through thick and thin, was meant to be their next phase of growth. Their promises to face life's challenges together seemed real, as they already had a glimpse of deep, abiding connection in the past, paving way for resilient couple, ready to weather the storms of life, emerging stronger with every upheaval.

Their love would 'age like fine wine', fermented with patience, compassion, compromise, and a mutual commitment to be together, forever…

What could be a better thing for Megha than to feel connected with Aayush for life, to know he was her biggest pillar of support, whom she could always rely upon, with the certainty of receiving pure love, always, the bedrock of their long-term relationship, gifting a sense of peace and fulfillment in the years to come.

*And how would they achieve it ? Simply by doing these 3 things:*

*First,* by tapping into their playfulness, the lighthearted, spontaneous energy, avoiding becoming too serious or monotonous, to keep the spark alive.

Going on regular date nights, planning staycations and couple holidays, doing fun activities together, exploring new avenues of shared interests, involving oneself into the likings of their partner, to keep their boat sailing.

Teasing and flirting, like the good old days, while making silly jokes, without the fear of being judged or mocked at, would help to maintain a cheerful, long-term relationship.

When life gets out of control, it's easy for couples to lose sight of the fun times they shared in the past, buried under the responsibilities piled up. Playful love will help to remind that laughter is the biggest medicine, an essential ingredient in the recipe for a healthy relationship.

*Second,* by being realistic, focusing on co-existing harmoniously, complementing each other's strengths and working towards mutual goals.

Pragmatic love is grounded in logic, and isn't driven just by intense passion or emotions alone, rather works on the principles of practicality. It will depend on how they both would fit in together, like the pieces of a jigsaw puzzle, develop compatibility with each other.

Being practical doesn't mean being unromantic, as the need of being spontaneous to keep the mood light and bring a smile on their partner's face during tough times, to help escape the daily life pressures of work and relish a better intimate experience will always be required.

Living together in real life is impacted by various factors like career plans, financial stability, one's own choices, family planning, belief system and personal values.

Hence, it will be critical to approach their relationship with an understanding to make it a win-win situation for both, forming the backbone of their successful tie-up, assuming they would love to tie knots in future.

Relationships that stand the test of time are created by striking a fine balance between emotional connection and practical decision-making.

Megha and Aayush would need to focus and comprehend where they are today, and where they would aspire to be, sharing themselves together in their personal life.

Its where the utmost important, the *third* step in building an enduring love will reveal its magic – the power of acceptance and forgiveness.

The most challenging, yet inevitable trait required at the end of both, is the ability to accept their partner to the fullest, as everyone comes as a package of both positive and negative qualities, good and bad habits.

Also, forgiving one's partner for mistakes and moving forward, together, without holding onto past hurt or feelings of resentment, is the recommended prescription by the doctors of love.

If there are no misunderstandings, hurt feelings, moments of doubt during conflicts, then such a relation or marriage isn't for real, but a myth.

Fights are inevitable, and avoiding discussions on working through issues won't help, instead, lead to more quarrel and disputes. Learning how to fight well will be the savior, and forgiveness will help rebuild trust and heal faster after the turbulent flight.

Forgiveness doesn't mean accepting intolerable behavior, or taking your partner for granted, assuming they will always forgive you, no matter how demeaned you make them feel due to your hurtful behavior.

Choosing their 'partner over pride' is forgiving love – which would allow every couple like Megha and Aayush to grow through hardship and experience enduring love.

Megha finally found an appropriate answer to the most burning question, that had been with her for so long – *What was love? Was it a virus or a vaccine?*

As she lay beside Aayush, she knew that her perception of love had changed completely.

Love, once a virus for her, was now a vaccine, a healing force that protected her heart, helped her revive, and created something beautiful, with all the nurturing by him.

Aayush was her vaccine, which healed the wounds left by Aryan, the virus of the past heartbreak, rebuilding her confidence and faith in love.

*Megha's thoughts discovered the idea built throughout her journey so far, that love could be both, a virus and a vaccine.*

Aayush finally woke up, looking at Megha's face, smiling deeply, reaching for her hand and holding her tight, said, "Oh you look so beautiful Megha, you're the best thing ever happened in my life."

Megha's heart full of emotions, covered his face gently with her curls, shading his eyes from the glare of sunlight.

As they kissed good morning to each other, she felt that the Cupid, the Roman God of love, had finally got its arrows shot spot on, making her fall in love with the perfect man; symbolizing the romantic spirit of Valentine.

It was a kiss that confirmed good times awaited ahead…

Love, sometimes like a wildfire, can burn your dreams, hopes and self-identity; like a phoenix, can also help you rise above from the ashes.

Like a paradox, love can be both beautiful and devastating in equal measure. Yes, it can really hurt, but can also heal. It could break you down, but also build you up. A risky affair or the safest place, one could ever find to reside.

It's all about where this energy is directed, leading to different outcome.

Just like power can run a heater or an air cooler, fire can give you warmth or burn the whole world down, water can produce electricity in a hydro plant or cause floods, air can run windmills or create havoc with cyclones, so can love with its enormous energy, lead to contrasting experiences, depending upon whom you're with in this romantic journey.

As a virus, love can make us cease to exist; as a vaccine, find the key to our heart, unlocking untapped possibilities to receive love and the hidden potential to gift in return; scripting a romantic tale to be remembered forever…

Until we meet again, I want you to reflect on your life, think about your past or ongoing relationship. How's your experience in your affair or marriage right now? Is your

*Love : Virus or Vaccine ?*

# Disclaimer

While this book draws inspiration from the real-life experiences of people around us, all the names, characters and places in this book are used in a fictious manner.

Any resemblance to actual persons, living or dead, or actual events is purely coincidental and unintentional.

Furthermore, the ideas, suggestions and action points suggested herein should not be used as a substitute for personal advice in any form whatsoever and each individual needs to exercise judgment and discretion in applying them in their own personal lives. It is advisable to reach out to a certified Life and Relationship Coach to discuss your own situation for a more fruitful outcome.

Point to Remember –

*While this Book talks about the story of a woman in love, all the 'good or bad' experiences shared throughout must be considered gender neutral; just like love is unisex & universal…*

# About the Author

Sandeep Bogra is a global multi-award-winning Life & Relationship Coach, Speaker & 2x Bestselling Author.

He was awarded as Best Life Coach, Speaker & Author by Bollywood Actor & Philanthropist, Sh. Sonu Sood at IGA Awards 2021, Goa (India), and regularly features as an Expert on TV channels on ET Now Swadesh, Zee Business & leading media publications globally.

He was also chosen as Life Coach of the Year at IMBC Awards 2021, Gurugram (India) organized by Action Coach USA, Franchise India & Entrepreneur magazine.

He has been recognized as one of the Top 20 Relationship Coaches worldwide by Coach Foundation and carries various other accolades under his name.

*A trusted Coach to Bollywood Celebs & Armed Forces.*

Being 'passionate about people' with his intention to add value to your life and relationships, Sandeep founded "Someone Listening" in 2008. He firmly believes that when something goes wrong, all you need to begin with, is an opportunity to speak your heart and feel understood by Someone, who Listens to you without any judgment, and guides you to have meaningful choices in life.

*A 'Catalyst for Change' for Clients from 30+ Countries...*

His Tailor-made Seminars and Key-note presentations influence your thinking-patterns and impacts lives positively, and undivided attention to your innermost feelings during One-on-One coaching, empowers you to make informed decisions and achieve results.

A Life Coach, certified from Tony Robbins – Madanes Training Center, USA; Neuro Linguistic Programming (NLP) Practitioner and an approved Counsellor. He is a Numerologist & also certified in Business Communication Skills from Dale Carnegie Institute.

Sandeep is also a Chartered Accountant from ICAI & an Executive MBA (Finance) from Institute of Management Technology, Ghaziabad. He started his career at McKinsey & Company and gained global Management Consulting experience in India & Middle East.

A dog-lover, philanthropist and an active member of Rotary International Club.

My Burning Desire:

"Touch & Transform Lives for the Better..."

www.ingramcontent.com/pod-product-compliance
Lightning Source LLC
Chambersburg PA
CBHW020606160726
47991CB00002B/895